HEROIC JOBS

MOUNTAIN RESCUE

Chris Oxlade

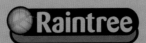
Raintree

Chicago, Illinois

www.capstonepub.com

Visit our website to find out more information about Heinemann-Raintree books.

To order:

☎ Phone 888-454-2279
 Visit www.capstonepub.com
to browse our catalog and order online.

Edited by Dan Nunn, Rebecca Rissman, and Catherine Veitch
Designed by Joanne Malivoire
Picture research by Elizabeth Alexander
Originated by Capstone Global Library
Printed and bound in China by CTPS

15 14 13 12 11
10 9 8 7 6 5 4 3 2 1

Library of Congress Cataloging-in-Publication Data
Oxlade, Chris.
  Mountain rescue / Chris Oxlade.
    p. cm.—(Heroic Jobs)
  Includes bibliographical references and index.
  ISBN 978-1-4109-4357-6 (hb)—ISBN 978-1-4109-4364-4 (pb) 1. Mountaineering—Search and rescue operations. I. Title.
  GV200.183.O97 2012
  363.14—dc22   2011015758

Acknowledgments
We would like to thank the following for permission to reproduce photographs: Alamy pp. 4 (© FORGET Patrick/SAGAPHOTO.COM), 6 (© Alaska Stock), 8 (© Caro), 9 (© FORGET Patrick/SAGAPHOTO.COM), 10 (© Ashley Cooper), 11 (© FORGET Patrick/SAGAPHOTO.COM), 14 (© Ashley Cooper), 19 (© blickwinkel), 20 (© Francesco Gavazzeni), 21 (© South West Images Scotland), 23 (© Ashley Cooper pics), 24 (© GAUTIER Stephane/SAGAPHOTO.COM), 26 (© Ashley Cooper), 29 (© Jeff Morgan 01); Corbis p. 16 (© John Van Hasselt); Photolibrary pp. 5 (Patrick Forget/Saga Photo), 7 (Matt Hage/Alaskastock), 12 (Patrick Forget/Saga Photo), 13 (Patrick Forget/Saga Photo), 15 (Patrick Forget/Saga Photo), 17 (Patrick Forget/Saga Photo), 22 (Hermes Images/Tips Italia), 27 (UWL/Imagebroker.net); Photoshot p. 25 (Paul Freytag); Shutterstock p. 18 (© amidala76).

Cover photograph of a rescuer searching for avalanche survivors reproduced with permission of Alamy (© FORGET Patrick/SAGAPHOTO.COM).

Every effort has been made to contact copyright holders of any material reproduced in this book. Any omissions will be rectified in subsequent printings if notice is given to the publisher.

We would like to thank Charley Shimanski for his invaluable help in the preparation of this book.

Some words are shown in bold, **like this**. You can find out what they mean by looking in the glossary.

Contents

Emergency!

High up on an icy mountainside a climber slips and twists his ankle. He can't climb up or down. The wind is howling and it's freezing cold. There's no time to lose. It's time to call for the mountain rescue team!

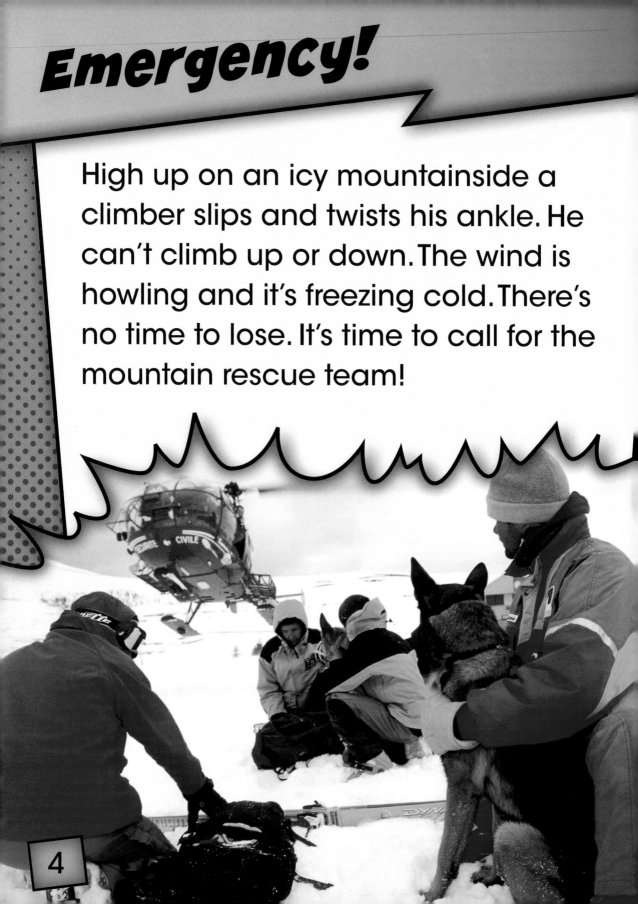

Mountain rescue teams are always ready to rescue people in danger.

Who Needs Help?

Hikers, mountaineers, rock climbers, skiers, and forest workers all play and work in the mountains. They need to be rescued if they get lost in bad weather, trapped on a cliff, injured in a fall, or become sick.

Sometimes people get buried in snow by **avalanches**.

Meet the Team

The members of a mountain rescue team are all expert mountaineers. Some of them are also experts in **first aid**. First aid is help given to an injured or sick person before they are taken to a hospital.

Did you know?
Mountain rescuers are often **volunteers**. When an emergency call comes they leave their normal jobs and rush to the rescue.

This rescuer is searching for people buried by an **avalanche**.

Helicopter Crews

Helicopter crews often help with rescues. Sometimes pilots have to hover just a few feet from cliffs in strong winds. The pilots need to be very skilled to do this.

winch

Did you know?
If a pilot can't find a
safe place to land,
rescuers can be
lowered to the ground
by a **winch**.

Dangers of the Job

Mountains can be dangerous places. Rescuers often have to climb up and down steep cliffs to reach injured people. The cliffs can be snowy and icy. It's often very windy, with heavy rain or snow, and very cold.

Did you know?
Rescuers often have to battle against strong winds at the tops of mountains.

Mountain Rescue Equipment

harness

rescue rope

stretcher

Rescue teams need special equipment. They have off-road trucks to travel into the mountains and take injured people to a hospital. They carry ropes, **harnesses**, and other equipment to climb cliffs and rescue people. They also stay in touch with each other and their base with walkie-talkie radios.

Mountain rescue teams always carry a **first aid** kit. They use dressings and bandages to treat cuts and strap up broken bones. They carry medicines to give to people who are sick.

Rescue Dogs

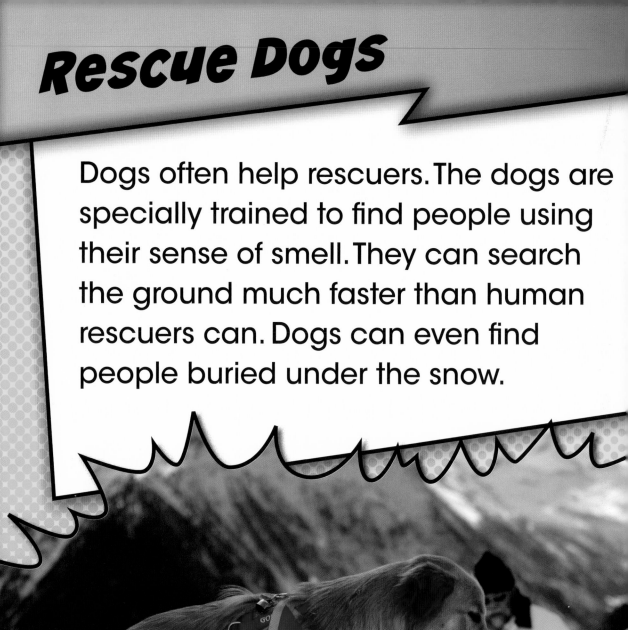

Dogs often help rescuers. The dogs are specially trained to find people using their sense of smell. They can search the ground much faster than human rescuers can. Dogs can even find people buried under the snow.

A rescue dog digs hurriedly in the snow to tell its handler that it has found somebody.

To the Rescue!

People who are lost or injured on a mountain call the rescue team by telephone or radio. They tell the team where they are and what injuries they have. The rescue team makes a rescue plan, gathers up their equipment, and sets off for the mountains.

Helicopter Rescue

Did you know?
On some rescue helicopters, the injured person is strapped onto a stretcher dangling below the helicopter!

Sometimes people are too sick or badly injured to walk to safety. The rescue team calls in a helicopter to pick up the injured person and take him or her to a hospital.

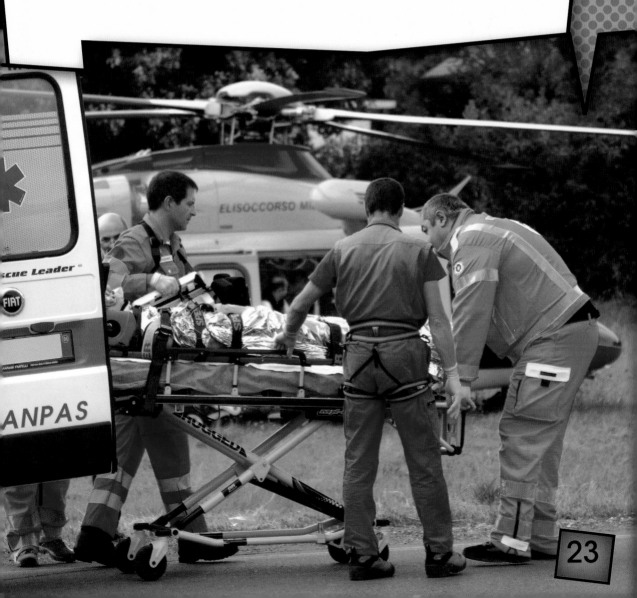

Avalanche Rescue

An **avalanche** sweeps away anything in its path. People can end up buried in snow where the avalanche stops. Rescuers sometimes push long sticks called avalanche probes into the snow. If the probe does not hit anything, then no one is buried there.

Did you know?
Avalanches can thunder downhill at speeds of more than 200 miles per hour.

Becoming a Rescuer

This rescuer is practicing first aid on a dummy.

Anybody who wants to be in a mountain rescue team must be an expert mountaineer. Rescuers have to be very fit. They must also know how to find their way in the mountains at night and in bad weather.

These rescuers are practicing rescuing a **casualty**.

27

Staying Safe in the Mountains

Hopefully you will never get into trouble on a mountain. Always follow this simple advice before you set off:

- Never go alone.
- Never go if bad weather is forecast.
- Always take warm clothes.
- Take emergency food and a first aid kit.
- Always tell somebody where you are going and what time you plan to be back.
- In an emergency call for help.

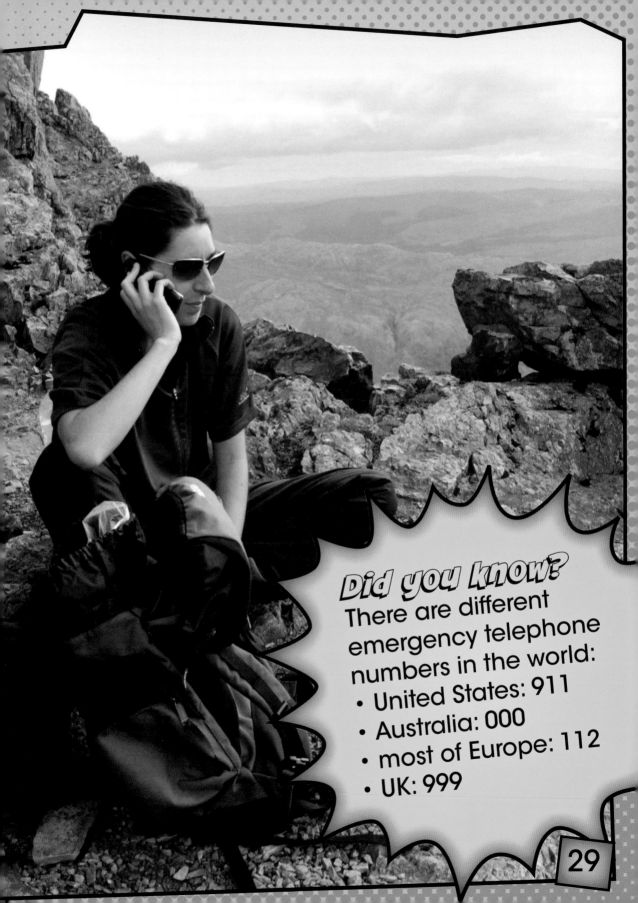

Did you know?
There are different emergency telephone numbers in the world:

- United States: 911
- Australia: 000
- most of Europe: 112
- UK: 999

Glossary

avalanche huge amount of snow and ice sliding down a mountainside

casualty someone who has been injured or killed

first aid help given to an injured or sick person before they can be taken to a hospital

harness straps that hold a person safely. The person can be picked up by a rope attached to the harness.

volunteer somebody who does not get paid for doing a job

winch machine that winds in or lets out wire. It can be used to lift people in and out of a helicopter.

Find Out More

Books

Anderson, Jameson. *Mountain Rescue Team.* Chicago: Raintree, 2007.

Murray, Julie. *Search-and-Rescue Animals.* Edina, Minn.: Abdo, 2009.

O'Shei, Tim. *Disaster in the Mountains!* Mankato, Minn.: Capstone Press, 2007.

Websites

jcsda.com/kids/index.html
Find out about search and rescue dogs with Hunter, the search and rescue dog.

www.mra.org
This is the website of the Mountain Rescue Association, one of the oldest search and rescue organizations in the United States.

www.sardogsus.org/
This is the website of Search and Rescue Dogs of the United States.

Index